2010 FANTASY FOOTBALL GUIDE

By

JAMES BUCKLEY JR.

**Beach
Ball
Books**

Published by

Beach Ball Books LLC

Santa Barbara, California

Book Design:

Bill Madrid

Production Manager:

Tina Dahl

Copy Editor:

Jim Gigliotti

Photos courtesy of:

AP Images

Illustrations by:

Mike Arnold, arnomation.com

ISBN: 978-1-936310-00-5

Printed in the United States.

CONTENTS

FOREWORD

WHAT A GREAT GAME!

*Back when I was a kid, playing wiffle ball in the streets and tackle foot-
ball in the snow was all part of the territory in my small Connecticut
town. Now there are realistic video games, the Internet, and countless
other technology-based hobbies to occupy your time until mom calls you
in at the end of the day. One of those hobbies is fantasy football.*

*If you're like me, you love sports—especially football and the
National Football League. And fantasy football is a little like owning
your very own NFL team. Some of my favorite players growing up were
Danny White, Tony Dorsett and Drew Pearson (yes, I was and still am a
huge Dallas Cowboys fan). I can't tell you how cool it would have been
to have those players on my very own fantasy team back then. Luckily,
you can! If you're a fan of the New Orleans Saints, how awesome would
it be to have Drew Brees as YOUR quarterback?*

*And you get to call the shots. You can add a player who's hot, you
can drop a player who's cold, and you can trade players just like the*

actual NFL teams do. Another great part of fantasy football is that you can play with your friends! That's right, the same pals you throw the football around with outside can play in your fantasy league.

Even now that I'm a "former kid," I still play in leagues with my best friends. And I couldn't enjoy it more, especially since I'm right in the middle of the fantasy-football buzz. I'm so blessed to be able to contribute to the success and popularity of fantasy football here at the NFL. I've even been able to get former greats like Dan Marino, Boomer Esiason, Marshall Faulk and Rod Woodson excited about playing fantasy football. What a thrill it's been, and the future is even more exciting with the release of NFL.com's new fantasy game. It has every single feature you want, including in-game video highlights of your favorite fantasy players. Why would you play anywhere else?

I hope you'll all join me in the wonderful world of NFL fantasy football! Good luck becoming a champion!

Michael Fabiano
NFL.com Fantasy Editor

KICKOFF!
AN INTRODUCTION

KICKOFF!

GETTING

DRAFTING

PLAYING

WINNING!

EXTRA

You're watching the third quarter of an NFL game between two teams—neither of which is your favorite. Suddenly, you leap from the sofa, screaming your head off! Your mother stares at you, your dog thinks you're crazy, and your sister runs screaming from the room! What happened to cause all this excitement?

For "regular" NFL fans, it might have been because their team just made a big play. But for fantasy football fans, all that screaming means that one of YOUR players just scored! That player got six points for the team that pays him every week. But he also got six points for **your** fantasy team!

And you get to scream dozens more times every Sunday afternoon if you play fantasy football. (Of course, you might also bury your head in sadness, but let's not think about that right now!) Every game becomes important to you and your fantasy team. The final extra point of the Monday-night game might be the difference between victory and . . . that other thing.

Fantasy football is a tremendous way to get even more fun out of your love of the NFL. You play with friends, you watch every game like a hawk (or should we say a Falcon?), and you get to "own," trade, and make deals with the superstars you love so much. NFL players are now used to kids greeting them with, "Hey, you're on my fantasy team!" (In fact, some NFL players are huge fantasy football fans; they get to "own" themselves . . . or trade themselves!)

If you're a rookie in fantasy football, don't worry! This guide will give you everything you need to know to create a team, pick the best players, and enjoy your season. If you're a fantasy vet, read on! Just because you've been playing for a couple of years doesn't mean you can't get better!

USING THIS GUIDE

Fantasy football has been around for a while, but it's never been easier to play. This guide will give you all the ins and outs of setting up a league and a team, choosing your players in the draft, and running your team all season long. From Kickoff Weekend through the final week of the NFL regular season, keep this book by your side. You'll find valuable tips on picking players, making deals, and winning!

Just because you know everything about football doesn't mean you know everything about fantasy football. But after you read this guide cover to cover . . . you'll know everything about both!

THE HISTORY OF FANTASY FOOTBALL

There's no truth to the rumor that President Franklin Roosevelt was very upset that he couldn't get Red Grange on his fantasy team. Though the NFL has been around since 1920, fantasy football has only been around for the past couple of decades. (In 1960, a group of writers in Oakland, California, created a league that was somewhat fantasy-like. However, it was called "GOPPL" for short and didn't really catch on.) The Internet made fantasy easy by letting team owners keep track of all the stats and results online. NFL.com has been offering fantasy football since 2000. In 2010, the league re-designed its entire fantasy game, adding video and special kids' sections.

KICKOFF!

GETTING

DRAFTING

PLAYING

WINNING!

EXTRA

POSITIONS

Throughout this book, we'll use these abbreviations for the positions so important to fantasy football:

QB = QUARTERBACK

RB = RUNNING BACK

WR = WIDE RECEIVER

TE = TIGHT END

K = KICKER

**D/ST = DEFENSE/
        SPECIAL TEAMS**

GETTING STARTED

WHAT IS FANTASY FOOTBALL?

Have you ever wanted your own football team? When you watch the NFL, do you yell at the TV? Do you watch your favorite team call a running play . . . when it should be calling for a pass? And do you like talking football with your friends?

Well, if you answered yes to any of those questions, then fantasy football is for you.

Fantasy football is a great way to enjoy your favorite sport, to make every NFL game you watch mean a lot, and to learn more about this great sport.

Fantasy football is basically this: You and your pals put together teams of real NFL players. Then, during real NFL games, you get the stats from those players. Those stats count for your fantasy team in head-to-head matchups with other fantasy teams in your league.

There's lots more to it than that, though!

You draft the team, you can trade players, you can pick up free agents, and, of course, you can talk smack with your fellow owners! Fantasy team owners love to keep track of several games at once, either on the  NFL Network or online at NFL.com, so they can keep an eye on all their players. And even if you don't have a player in an NFL game that you're watching, you might have an opponent's player to watch . . . and hope he doesn't do too well!

KICKOFF!

GETTING STARTED

DRAFTING

PLAYING

WINNING!

EXTRA

Do you have favorite players? You can try to get them on your team. Fantasy team owners who draft their faves get to cheer twice—once for their NFL team and again for their fantasy team!

How cool is this? You don't have to just watch Drew Brees throw a touchdown pass for the Saints . . . you can watch him throw for six for YOUR team. When you see Larry Fitzgerald's diving catch, it will be a score for the Cardinals . . . and for YOU! And that long field goal that wins a game for the Packers might also win a game for YOU!

REALITY FOOTBALL

This book is about how to play and win at fantasy football. But it's all based on "reality" football. That is, you can't have fantasy football without all the awesome games played each week by the athletes of the NFL. In various places in this book, look for boxes labeled "Reality Football." These will give you insider information on some cool NFL stuff, plus show you other ways that fantasy football mirrors "real" life in the NFL, on the field and in the front office.

Fun for 17 Weeks!

Fantasy football doesn't happen just on Sunday (or Monday night!). Fantasy football goes on all season long, week after week. You have to stay on top of all the latest player moves, just like a real team's general manager. You need to watch for big trades or injuries, or find out when a team is changing its playbook.

After the first 12 or 14 weeks, most fantasy football leagues have playoffs, before the "real" NFL playoffs. Usually, the top four teams make the playoffs, so you've got a good chance to try for the trophy. There are some great tips about surviving the playoffs on page 72.

Fantasy football can take over your life if you're not careful . . . then again, maybe that's not a bad thing!

Why Stop at 17?

Fantasy leagues usually stop after the NFL regular season. Why is that?

There's one simple reason: Only 12 teams make the NFL playoffs while fantasy owners can have players on any of the 32 teams. So, if the fantasy playoffs went into January, too, fantasy owners who have players that are on non-playoff teams might not have enough players!

There is an option, however. NFL.com and other sites let you start new fantasy leagues using only players on playoff teams. So while your "regular" fantasy season might be over, maybe you can try fantasy playoff football!

I DRAFTED MYSELF!

Football fans are not the only people who love fantasy football. NFL players themselves are big fans. Since fantasy football started, many NFL players have owned fantasy teams. They play with and against friends, family, and teammates. Just like fantasy owners at home, they study the stats, draft their teams, and make moves just like their own general managers and coaches. The only difference is that they can be friends with their own fantasy players . . . or even draft themslves!

In 2009, running back Leon Washington, then of the Jets, won a fantasy football league made

NFL player and fantasy owner Chris Cooley.

up of all NFL players. No surprise here: Washington had the Jets defense on his fantasy team! Some of the players in that league and others have a unique way to play: They draft themselves! Washington called his own number in his league's draft . . . and then benched himself for his own championship game! That's right. With a chance to put himself into the starting line-up for his fantasy championship, Washington saw that his opponent DeAngelo Williams of the Panthers had put himself on the bench. That meant that Williams knew he wouldn't be playing for Carolina, so Washington picked up Carolina backup Jonathan Stewart. Stewart had a big game in place of Williams, and the move helped Leon's "Jet Lizzie" team win it all!

In other fun NFL player moves, Bears running back Matt Forté chose his Chicago teammate Robbie Gould as his fantasy kicker one season. Of course, that meant Gould could not choose himself for his own team!

Washington tight end Chris Cooley is a longtime fantasy fan. He has written blogs and magazine articles about his love for fantasy. Chris actually has faced both sides of an unusual fantasy situation. In a 2005 game, he caught three TD passes for the Redskins. His fantasy team lost, however, since his opponent that week had a certain Washington tight end on his team. That's right: Reality Cooley played against Fantasy Cooley!

BE THE COMMISSIONER!

If you REALLY love fantasy football, you can take NFL Commissioner Roger Goodell's job. Well, not really, but you can be the commish of your own fantasy league. As the commissioner, you make decisions like what scoring rules to use, where to hold the draft, and who to invite into the league. Of course, this also means you have to be fair to all the owners and not favor one over another. You also have to settle any disagreements that owners have over players or rules. But since you're a football expert—and a wonderful person, right?—then this won't be a problem for you!

It's sort of like being the captain of a sports team. You still have to play the game, play by the same rules, and do your part to help your team succeed. But as captain, the other players look to you for leadership. They follow your example. In the case of fantasy football, this might mean proposing fair trades, not hiding information, or making sure everyone is receiving all the league news.

We all want to win our fantasy games and our league, but commissioners want everyone to have a good time, too. That doesn't mean losing, it just means being honest and fair.

THE COMMISH.

Okay, that's the boring parent stuff. Here's the fun part: It's good to be the king! (Or the queen, of course!) Being in charge of a league means you can gather your best friends, you can have the draft in your basement, and you can be in charge of naming the league (see page 21).

In this guide, you'll see lots of tips for people who actually form leagues, as well as for regular fantasy players. If you decide to take on this big job . . . good luck! We're here to help!

TIP FROM THE PRO!

Michael Fabiano is the fantasy editor for NFL.com. He's been playing fantasy football since before you were born! He's been the commissioner of dozens of leagues. Here are some tips from this national expert on how to be a good commish:

"The most important thing is to be fair. Don't make decisions that would benefit your team or your friend's team. Make it fun for everyone. Also, make sure to know the owners. If they are new to fantasy, help them learn the rules and about how to move and trade players. Finally, make sure all the rules are set before the season; it's hard to make changes once you start playing. Being the commissioner should add to your fun, not take away from it. Enjoy it!"

SETTING UP A TEAM AND A LEAGUE

GETTING STARTED!

When fantasy football started, team owners had to do all the math and counting by themselves. Owners still drafted teams and then watched the NFL to see how their teams did. But they had to add all the stats and points by themselves, and keep track of their league standings from week to week. Owners kept big notebooks and read magazines and looked at tons of newspapers. The Internet wasn't really "on" back then, so fantasy owners had to work a lot harder!

Today, of course, it's a snap. By playing fantasy football online (on NFL.com, we hope!), you can let the computer do the heavy lifting . . . while you have all the fun! NFL.com and other Web sites keep track of your teams, your league games, the scores, and the stats. They also provide tons of research and information all season long so you can make good choices to improve your team. You can find out which tight end to start against the Bengals this weekend or

which wide receiver has the best chance for a breakout season. Need to find out the latest news about who's starting and who's not? Your league's Web page will have the answer. (Of course, your football knowledge will be important, too. Remember, you're the owner . . . the decisions are yours!)

Setting Up a League

To set up a league, sign up online (be sure to ask Mom and Dad first). The Web site will let you pick a name for your league and your teams. Most Web sites have a basic game that has all the rules set. Make sure you read them over, whether you are a player or a commissioner.

If you are the commish (see page 16), you can also set up different rules for your league on most sites. Among the rules you can can choose for your league:

- How many teams can be in the league.
- How the teams are split into divisions.
- What positions each team needs to fill (some leagues allow a "flex" player who can be a RB or WR).
- What sort of scoring system you want to use (see page 25 for scoring basics).
- How your league playoffs will work.
- When your draft will be held (there are lots of ways to draft; see page 28).
- Where your draft will be held (online or in person).
- What snacks to bring to the draft! (Though they won't be online!)

KICKOFF

GETTING STARTED

DRAFTING

PLAYING

WINNING

EXTRA

Once you have entered all your league's team names and set the rules, your league is ready to go. You can send emails to all your league's owners or else just tell your friends where to log on. There is usually a message board on the site. The commissioner can send notes to all the league owners. That might include info on new rules, dates and times of the draft, or ideas about how to get together to watch the Kickoff Weekend games in the days after the draft.

With all your league's owners on board and a draft day set up on your site, you're almost ready for the season. However, as a team owner, you've got a lot of information to gather on top players at each position. You'll look at Web sites, read magazines, watch TV sports shows, and talk with fellow football fanatics. You'll spend hours debating who the best tight end is or which running back is ready to bust out with a high-scoring season.

It will take hours and drive your parents crazy (unless one of them is in the league with you!). But that's the fun part!

NAMING YOUR LEAGUE

Each fantasy league gets a name . . . and you get to decide what it is. You might use the name of your school, your town, or your favorite NFL team. You can make up a weird name or use some fun phrase from a TV show or video game. Or you can dig into your favorite list of NFL slang. Be creative! Have fun with it! No one wants to play in a fantasy league with a boring name!

Some ideas (but you can do better, right?):

POWERFUL PACKERS PLAYERS

ARIZONIACS

RED ZONE RENEGADES

THE WHEEZERS

THE KIDS ARE ALL RIGHT

THEY COULD GO ALL THE WAY!

NAMING YOUR TEAM

Just like you want your league to have a cool name, you want your team name to be memorable, too. This name represents you, so think of something you love. Are you a cookie fiend? Try "The Cookie Monsters." Do you like skateboarding? You could own "Ollie's Tailgrabs." Are you a great passer and a robot maker? Become "The Quarterbackatrons." Try puns with your name. How about: "The Nick of Times," "The FootballiStans," or the "LomBartis"? Your fantasy Web site will limit the number of characters, but within that limit, go wild . . . be brave . . . be funny. And pick a winner!

THE QUARTERBACK-ATRONS

THE FOOTBALLISTANS

LOMBARTIS

THE NICK OF TIMES

THE COOKIE MONSTERS

OLLIE'S TAILGRABS

KICKOFF

GETTING STARTED

DRAFTING

PLAYING

WINNING

EXTRA

🏈 REALITY FOOTBALL

NAME THAT TEAM!

You'll come up with your own awesome name for your fantasy team. But how did some NFL teams come up with the names they use?

Arizona Cardinals: The Cardinals first played in Chicago in 1899! The owner got a shipment of jerseys that he thought would be maroon. When he saw them, he said, "Those are cardinal red." And the name stuck.

Green Bay Packers: The team was started by the Indian Packing Co. in Green Bay, which packed fish from the Great Lakes. They added the city name in 1920.

Pittsburgh Steelers: The team was founded in 1933 as the Pirates, but changed in 1940 to a name that called to mind the many steel factories in this Pennsylvania city.

San Francisco 49ers: The Niners were named for California settlers who came west during the 1849 Gold Rush.

Tennessee Titans: When the Houston Oilers moved to Tennessee in 1997, at first they kept their nickname. But in 1999, they were renamed for a race of giants from Greek mythology. (They couldn't be "Giants" . . . that one's taken!)

KICKOFF!

GETTING STARTED

DRAFTING

PLAYING

WINNING!

EXTRA

HEY, WANNA PLAY?

If you have eight or ten pals who love football, this part is easy. But if you don't have enough and need to recruit some fantasy players to fill up your league, here are some good reasons you can give them to play:

- New ways to brag about your football knowledge.

- You get to tell Peyton Manning and Adrian Peterson what to do! (Well, sort of . . .)

- Every late-season game between two last-place NFL teams will be really important now!

- Age does not matter; kids often beat dads in fantasy football!

- Real NFL owners have to have a lot of money; you can own your fantasy team for free!

- Pick players from your favorite teams . . . and root for them twice as hard!

- You can't beat me in real foot-ball, why not try to beat me in fantasy?

SCORING SYSTEMS

Knowing how to score points in fantasy football is an important part of owning a fantasy team. It's not as easy as just looking at the scoreboard (though NFL.com does have an awesome in-game fantasy scoreboard, complete with video of all the scoring plays by your fantasy team!). Players can score fantasy points for your team in many different ways, including touchdowns, field goals, rushing yards, passing yards, and even interceptions and sacks. You add up all those points, then match your total against your fantasy opponent for the weekend. The winner of the game is the team with the most fantasy points.

The following pages show a fairly standard way that fantasy points are added up. However, make sure you learn your own league's rules. Knowing how to set up your team to maximize your points is key to becoming a fantasy champion.

CHANGE IT UP!

On most fantasy Web sites, you can "customize" your league. That is, you can change some of the scoring rules to match up with what you and your friends like. You can make touchdown passes worth four points or six points. You can give more points to defenses for tackles or turnovers. You can award points to receivers for their receptions, not just for yardage and touchdowns. Some leagues let you gain points for return yards. Be creative!

QBs

4 or **6** points for a TD pass
6 points for a TD run
1 point for each 25 passing yards
1 point for each 10 rushing yards
-2 points for an interception or a lost fumble

RBs

6 points for a TD run or catch
1 point for each 10 rushing yards
1 point for each 10 receiving yards
-2 points for a lost fumble

WRs

6 points for a TD catch or run
1 point for each 10 receiving yards
1 point for each 10 rushing yards
-2 points for a lost fumble

TEs

6 points for a TD catch or run

I point for each 10 receiving yards

I point for each 10 rushing yards

-2 points for a lost fumble

K

I point for a successful point after touchdown

3 points for a field goal up to 49 yards

5 points for a field of 50-plus yards

Note: Some leagues break it down by other yardage levels.

D/ST

6 points for a touchdown via return
  (interception, fumble, kickoff, punt)

2 points for a safety

2 points for an interception

2 points for a fumble recovery

I point for a sack

Defenses also get points depending on how many points
or how few yards they allow.

Note: Some leagues also give points for tackles or return yards.

DRAFTING A TEAM

WHAT IS THE DRAFT?

Just as teams do in the NFL, you'll start your fantasy football team by holding a draft. NFL teams choose college players; you'll choose NFL players.

Fantasy football drafts can take many forms, but the basic way is this: You get together with all the owners in your league. You take turns choosing NFL players. Each team has to have players at all the positions. You can decide how many players to draft, but it's usually 14-16 per team. You'll end up with at least one player for each position, plus backups at key positions.

Draft Day is, for many owners, one of their favorite days of the year. You get to spend a couple of hours talking football with your pals. And you get a chance to have your favorite NFL stars play for the Amazing Cheeseheads of Washington School (or whatever cool name you came up with for your team).

Many fantasy fans make Draft Day a special event, holding it somewhere interesting. Many adult fans travel together to a hotel or resort. You probably won't do that, but see who had the coolest rec room or basement. Set up some tables and put name cards in front of each owner. Maybe you can even design helmets or stickers with your team's logo!

As much fun as Draft Day is, however, you can't just show up and pick players and hope to win. You have some work to do, Fantasy Fan, to get ready. Winning fantasy means knowing more about the NFL than the other owners in your league.

IT STARTS WITH RESEARCH

To succeed in the NFL, players must have skills, strength, and determination. But they also have to work hard year-round to train their bodies to get ready for the season. Fantasy team owners don't need strength (unless you wrestle your buddies to see who gets first pick), but they do have to work hard before the first game. The preseason hard work is research. The more information you can gather about players and teams, the better chance your fantasy team will have for success. Going into a draft without research would be like showing up for a football game without your helmet!

Here are some key things to watch for when you're researching which NFL players to target in the draft:

Know your league's rules! Make sure you know how points are scored so you can look for players who score those points! That is, if touchdown passes are worth less than touchdown runs, perhaps a running back is more valuable to you. Or do defenses in your league get extra points for a low number of yards allowed?

Watch for player movement: A player scores points for you by himself, but the team he's on has a lot to do with that.

A very skilled receiver who has moved to a team with an inexperienced quarterback might have lost value. Or a QB moving to a team with great receivers jumps in value.

- Preseason games: Don't look too closely at preseason stats. Most teams only play their stars for a short time so that they can look at other players and to avoid injuries. So if a Pro Bowl runner only gains 27 yards in an August game, don't downgrade him for the regular season!

- Make lots of lists: Try to have a list of at least 15 quarterbacks and 30-40 running backs and wide receivers. Those are the key positions and the more you know about them, the better. You can use rankings from experts (see box on "research help" and the rankings on page 81) or make your own. Remember, you're not looking for how a player did last year, you're using information to predict how a player will do *this* year! You might need a crystal football to help, but if you gather enough facts, you'll be ready to become a fantasy champion.

KICKOFF

GETTING

DRAFTING A TEAM

PLAYING

WINNING!

EXTRA

RESEARCH HELP

Web sites: Well, of course, NFL.com is the best place to get your fantasy info. There are lots of others out there, but, you know, we think we're No. 1.

Magazines: Magazines are handy ways to get lists of players, often ranked by the experts. But make sure and check for the latest player movements on NFL.com.

Newspapers (you know, those things some of your parents used to read!): Just before the NFL season, newspapers include fantasy and "reality" previews. Look for players who have moved teams. Their new teams might make them much better fantasy choices than their old teams.

TV: The NFL Network is one of many sports cable channels that covers fantasy football. The experts on their shows talk to coaches, general managers, and players all the time. They can sometimes share inside information on a team's plans that might help you discover a "sleeper" (a surprise starter) or to watch for a rising young star.

WHAT'S A MOCK DRAFT?

The word "mock" means, in this case, something that is not real. You'll find lots of mock fantasy drafts as you get ready for your own. In these pretend drafts, experts do an entire draft. Their choices and ideas can help you plan your own draft. For example, if all the mock drafts you see have a quarterback taken first overall, that might be a clue for you. Or if you see a certain player going much later than you thought, he might be a great surprise pick for you to make . . . or not! Look for mock drafts on NFL.com and in fantasy magazines.

NFL Commissioner Roger Goodell with 2010 No. I draft pick Sam Bradford of St. Louis.

GET READY TO DRAFT!

Sometimes the hardest thing about Draft Day is agreeing with your fellow owners on when to have it! If you all go to the same school, maybe you can get together at lunch or right after school. Ask your teacher if you can use a room at school, or just gather at a picnic table on the playground. Make sure everyone will be able to stay for the entire draft.

You can also host Draft Day at your house. Then your parents can help with snacks and you'll have a nice big table to sit around while you do the draft. Rent a football movie or a Super Bowl highlight video to watch afterward!

Drafts can also be held online. (NFL.com is a great place to do this.) With your parents' permission, you can get your league together online. The Web site keeps track of all the players chosen and helps you find players who haven't been picked yet. You can prepare your own personal rankings of players ahead of time, too. During the draft, you can put players in a line so that when it's your turn, you're ready with your choices.

Remember that on most sites, there is a time limit for each pick. If you only have 60 seconds or 90 seconds to choose, you better have a couple of players ready. If you don't and the computer picks for you, you never know who you'll get!

Most sites have message boards so you can make jokes and ask questions during the Draft. An online draft is also a great way to play fantasy football with friends and relatives who live in other cities. See if you can get all your cousins to play in a league together!

DRAFT ORDER

 If this is your first year, just picking names out of a hat works just fine.

 If you're a veteran league, consider picking in reverse order of last year's standings; that's how the NFL does it!

 Have someone outside the league make up a 10-question NFL trivia quiz; then rank the draft in order of how many questions owners got right!

THE SNAKE

Once you have the draft order, make sure everyone agrees to the "snake" format. That's a great way to make sure that everyone gets a fair shot at a good team. In this method, in a 10-team league the first round is 1 through 10. Then the second round is 10 through 1. The third round goes back to 1 through 10, and so on. That is, after Owner No. 10 makes his first pick, he'll get another pick that's the first of the second round. Think of this draft order like a snake moving back and forth (or up and down), and it'll make sense.

THE RULES

Make sure that everyone knows what the position rules for your league will be. In some leagues, you can play two quarterbacks each week. In others, you can have a "flex" position. That is, you can add another running back or wide receiver each week. Knowing what positions will be key in your league will guide people in the draft. There's nothing worse than finishing a draft and realizing you needed two more running backs!

TIME LIMITS

Drafts can go on for hours and hours . . . unless you have a time limit. Decide together how much time an owner gets to make his or her pick. Maybe it's three minutes after the previous pick . . . or 90 seconds.

The early rounds will go pretty quickly, but later rounds can slow down as owners look for gems and hidden sleepers.

SNACKS!

Of course, sitting around talking about football for a couple of hours is hungry work! Having snacks on hand will make your day more fun . . . and filling. Of course, we should mention the healthy ones first, such as raisins or trail mix or fruit or yogurt. But we all know what you're going to have on the table, right? Just don't get chip crumbs in your laptops.

CHEAT SHEETS

You can't take a cheat sheet with you to school for a math test. In fantasy football, however, it's okay to have one on Draft Day. Cheat sheets are lists of players you want to draft. You rank them according to how much you want them. Some owners make lists that include all the players. Others make a list for each position. However you do it, they're a handy way to keep track of who has been drafted . . . and who you want to draft. The lists in the color section at the back of this book are a great place to start making your own cheat sheets.

QB
1. Joe Montana
2. Johnny Unitas
3. Bart Starr

RB
1. Jim Brown
2. Gale Sayers
3. Emmitt Smith

WR
1. Jerry Rice
2. Don Hutson

DRAFT DAY!

"With the first pick of our fantasy draft, I choose . . ."

With those words, your fantasy draft is underway. Owners take turns choosing the players they want. (See how long it takes for the someone to say, "Oh, man, I was just going to pick him!") In the meantime, try to have three or four players in mind so that when it's your turn, you'll have a name ready to go, even if someone has indeed just picked your top choice.

Round and round the draft will go. Watch carefully how things are going. If you see that everyone is snapping up wide receivers early, you might want to either join them or wait until later. By choosing another position, you might be able to get a higher-ranked player. Don't be bothered by "runs." That is, when two or three owners pick a tight end one after the other. Stick to your research and your plan.

However, the other thing to remember is: Don't be afraid to change your plan. If it gets to your turn and you see that one of your top picks is available, even if you have someone else at that position . . . grab him. Remember, if you have several top players at one position, you might be able to trade one later (see page 58).

KEEPING TRACK

Using your cheat sheets or whatever lists you've made up, keep track of what players have been selected. If you have a time limit, you don't want to run out of time naming players and having everyone shout,

"Taken!" over and over. Many fantasy owners keep lists by position and cross off players as they are chosen. That way, when it's your turn and you know you need to pick a wide receiver, you can go to that list and find your pick.

LATE-ROUND "STEALS"

Just about every fantasy season, a player chosen late in the draft has a big impact on many teams. In 2009, Dallas wide receiver Miles Austin was probably not even chosen in many fantasy leagues, but by the end of the year, he was a big fantasy star. Finding those "hidden gems" late in the draft can often be the difference between winning a championship and . . . not.

Don't stop paying attention after all the "big names" are chosen. Look for young, rising stars to give your team depth. Is there a top player coming back from an injury that was doing well before he was hurt? Is there a young player stepping up into a starting role on a very solid team? Did a second-year player start to really come on late in his rookie year? All those can be clues to finding what fantasy fans call "sleepers."

WRAPPING IT UP

When the draft is finished, make sure that everyone has filled all the positions they need. Then the commissioner will enter the teams onto the Web site, if you haven't done the draft online. Then it's time to look at your team and see how your draft went. Draft Day is a big part of fantasy football, but the real work starts now: Playing the season. Read on starting on page 50 for extensive tips on having a great fantasy football season.

READING OTHER OWNERS

When NFL teams play, they study their opponents for days. They learn as much as they can about the team they will play. They look for weaknesses and strengths. They come up with plans to take advantage of those weaknesses. You can do something like that in your fantasy draft. If you know that that kid Tommy from down the block loves the Cowboys, you can make sure to remind him about Dallas players when it's his turn. Maybe he'll pick one and leave another player that you want out there for you to choose. Or another owner is a wide receiver on his pee-wee team. Chances are he'll pay more attention to wide receivers for fantasy.

On the other hand, knowing your fellow owners' favorite teams can help you later in the year. If you know your brother LOVES the Cardinals, pick an Arizona running back BEFORE your brother can. Guess who you'll be able to trade with later in the year!

Another thing you can "steal" is a handcuff. That is, if an owner chooses a team's No. 1 running back, you can use a late-round pick to choose that team's No. 2. If No. 1 suffers an injury, that No. 2 will suddenly be very valuable.

Doing well in the draft often means knowing your fellow owners as well as you know the NFL players you're choosing.

DRAFT DAY LINGO

Here are some words that you'll probably hear bounce around your draft day table:

Bye week: the week an NFL team doesn't play; not a good idea to have lots of players with the same bye week.

Flex: some leagues offer a roster spot that can be used by a RB or WR or TE, depending on what the owner wants.

Flier: a draft pick that's a bit of a reach, a player who might be a star or a big bust.

Handcuff: if you pick up a huge star, pick up his backup in case of injury.

Reach: a player that most people expect to have a poor season, but that you pick hoping for the best!

Sleeper: a player that you snag whom no one expects to be a star, but who turns out to score tons of points.

Serpentine: the order of most fantasy drafts; also known as the "snake" draft. It moves back forth in order so that the order of picks is reversed each round (see page 35).

POSITION TIPS

Every season brings a new crop of NFL stars at each position. But each position has some key skills and stats you should look at as you consider which players to draft.

QUARTERBACK

No surprises here: You want big stars. Look for high passing-yardage totals and lots of TD passes. Year after year, there are a handful of players you can expect to be at the top of the quarterback rankings. However, if you have 10 teams in your league, only three or four of you will get the top passers. So your key is to find those other passers who are on the rise and who will join that elite group.

Teams that throw the ball a lot are a great place to start. If a team has a great running game, then their QB probably won't throw a lot of passes. For the most part, a team with a young passer also won't provide you with a lot of fantasy points.

Does a team have a great group of receivers? A passer new to that team might not click with those receivers right away, but after a few weeks, watch for his numbers to rise . . . and grab him.

Have a choice between two great passers? Pick the one who has thrown fewer interceptions. Remember that in most scoring systems you lose points for picks.

Passing is on the rise in the NFL. In recent seasons, more and more passers have racked up big numbers. It's one of the two most important fantasy positions, so make sure and spend time finding a great QB.

QB Tips:

- Few great fantasy QBs play for struggling teams; look for wins!
- Look for a solid backup in later rounds.
- Avoid QBs who play for teams with offenses based more heavily on running.

RUNNING BACKS

A few years ago, most draft experts said to always choose two running backs before you chose any other players. That's changed a lot. Today, most experts say you need a dominant QB and a top RB as your first two picks.

Finding that top RB is harder than it used to be. Many NFL teams rely on two or three backs now instead of handing the rock to one guy. Those teams with one lead RB are the places you should look first for your runners.

Look for a running back who gets most of his team's carries. Find the guy who gets those carries AND who gets the goal-line rushes that turn into touchdowns. And seek out a running back who also gets a lot of receptions, perhaps 50 or more per season. Got him? Well, grab him and hold on if you find him!

As great as that runner sounds—lots of carries, goal-line work, great hands—there are usually now only a small corps of such players. More and more teams are using a "running back by committee." That is, they use one guy for regular runs, another for third-down passing plays, and a third for short-yardage plunges. Trying to figure out which of those three will score the most fantasy points is like throwing darts. You might get lucky . . . or you might get shut out.

So the key for running backs: Target the ones who get the most carries. They'll have the most chances to be productive.

RB Tips:

- **Great hands?** A good second RB on your team might be one who racks up receiving yards.

- **TD machines.** Another good second RB is one of those short-yardage specialists. As an example, in 2006, Marion Barber of the Cowboys had only 654 yards, but he scored 14 touchdowns, most on short runs.

- **Watch for tired players.** The year or two after a player racks up 350 or more touches can sometimes mean a slow-down in production.

KICKOFF!

GETTING

DRAFTING
A TEAM

PLAYING

WINNING!

EXTRA

WIDE RECEIVERS

This is a category in which watching the waiver wire often pays off big. (For more on picking up players during the season, see page 52.) During the draft, you can target the three or four players who are expected to rack up lots of TD catches and receiving yards. There are always an elite group of such players, and that group doesn't change much from year to year. However, in most years, after those first small handful of stars, you can find a lot of solid receivers.

In 2009, for example, while many fantasy owners chased superstars like Randy Moss or Chad Ochocinco, owners who waited and snagged Miles Austin ended up with more points. In the draft, look to find that top QB and an all-around running back before you try to snag your top receiver.

This is also a category in which you'll often find young players emerging suddenly. A quarterback and a receiver can take weeks (or years) to learn to connect. When they do, though, it can mean big points for them . . . and you! Watch for young receivers who become their passer's top target.

A team's offensive strategy is also a good way to spot receivers. If a team has a great passer and loves to throw the ball, players on that team are more likely to emerge as points-producing machines.

TIGHT END

Most fantasy owners don't pay much attention to this position. However, owning a solid tight end can really help your team.

In recent years, many NFL offenses have increased their use of the tight end. As more and more teams pass more and more often, the TE has become a bigger part of many offenses. Antonio Gates set a record for touchdowns by a TE in 2007 with 11. But that record lasted only two years until Vernon Davis broke it with 13 in 2009! And Davis was not alone that year; seven TEs had at least 7 TDs.

Most teams will feature one player as their pass-catching TE. Make sure the tight end you choose is not used most often as a blocker. Also, look for teams that do use the TE in their offense. Some teams still focus their passing games on wide receivers, with TEs being used more often as decoys.

If you don't land a big tight end in the draft, pay attention as the season goes on. It's not unusual for surprise players to pop up in this category. Be the first in your league to spot them!

KICKERS

Is there any fantasy football position harder to predict than kicker? Every year, it seems like one kicker will be the top guy at his position . . . and every year, some other guy emerges to be No. 1.

Most fantasy owners pick their kicker last in the draft. They also expect to change that kicker many times during the season.

It's hard to know when a kicker will have a big game, but there are some keys to finding the right kicker each week:

Domes: Kickers often have more success indoors, where the wind can't affect their kicks.

Weather: Late in the season, bad weather makes kicking tricky; look for kickers playing in warm weather.

Opponent: Does a team have a stiff defense that doesn't give up a lot of TDs? That can turn into more chances for field-goal tries.

Offense: A low-scoring, ball-control team won't have a high-scoring kicker. A pass-happy, high-scoring team probably will. Follow the points!

Distance: Some kickers excel at those high-scoring long FGs. If you have a choice between two equal kickers, pick the strongest leg.

DEFENSE/SPECIAL TEAMS

This is the secret stockpile of fantasy points. A really great defense can score fantasy points for you in many ways, from turnovers to shutouts to an exciting "pick six." (That's an interception returned for a touchdown.) Add in the possible points from an exciting return man and you've got a victory-making combo.

Defense is another position, like kicker, where you'll probably switch around a lot. Look at the matchups each week. You'll often see that some NFL teams are really struggling to score points. Guess what? The defense that will face them on Sunday has a pretty good chance to rack up some fantasy points!

Watch how defenses are doing in the early weeks. Are they racking up turnovers? Does their secondary seem like they always are heading for the end zone? Track down these teams and make them your own.

As for returns, a few players often stand out from the rest. If their team's defenses are halfway decent, that can make for a points-happy pairing.

PLAYING THE GAME

Time to Play!

Drafting your fantasy football team is only the first small step to creating a winning fantasy season. The draft is an important step, of course, and you should work hard to do the best job you can on Draft Day. However, the work (and the fun!) doesn't stop once you've closed your cheat sheets and draft lists. Like an NFL team, Kickoff Weekend is just the beginning . . . the daily and weekly fun of fantasy football goes on throughout the regular season.

With the draft completed, it's time to really turn on the jets and think like an NFL general manager. Those guys spend 18 hours a day thinking about how they can make their teams better. While you won't have that much time (there's that whole "school" thing to consider, and you've got to eat, right?), you can use your time to learn more about the players in the league and how you can make your team into a winner. This chapter includes information about how you can add and change players and how you can arrange your players each week.

Your tools will include NFL.com (of course!), team Web sites, newspapers, magazines, and TV reports. But all that is just information. They won't give you the answers. Like that NFL general manager, it's up to YOU to make the decisions. Make the right ones, and you'll be dancing around in December. We won't even talk about making the wrong ones!

FREE AGENTS

A free agent is a player in fantasy football (or reality football; see page 54) who is not under contract to a team. That is, he can sign with any team he wants. In fantasy, free agents are players who were not chosen during the draft. Since you're the boss of your team, you choose all the players, including free agents. You can add those free agents to your team throughout the season. Pay attention to choosing free agents: This is the best way to improve your team!

Finding the right free agents means paying attention to changes in NFL teams as the season moves along. Is a team passing more often? Is a young player moving into a starting role? Is a veteran having trouble so that a backup is getting more playing time? Watch the stats and results each week and look for these players.

Look for a team that will be facing several weaker opponents. Players on that team might be in for good weeks. What about a defense that is facing a low-ranked team? Selecting that defense and adding it to your roster could mean big points. Searching for another wide receiver? Check out the passing stats and see if a quarterback has been hot; chances are his receivers are moving up, too. If you're looking to add a running back, try finding some team's goal-line specialist. They're often on the free-agent list and will score touchdowns, if not rack up lots of rushing yards.

The search for free agents will take up a bunch of your time during the season. But when you discover that running back who suddenly busts out for three touchdowns the week after he joins your team in Week 7 . . . all your hard work will pay off!

CLAIMING FREE AGENTS

How do you add free agents to your team? It takes good research, good timing, and, yes, a little luck.

If you play on NFL.com, you claim a free agent simply by going to the site and looking at a list of such players. You can search by position or by points scored or by NFL team. Once you find a player that you want, select the player and click that you want to add him. You'll also have to drop a player, since you can only have a set number of players on your team (each league is different, but it's usually 14-16 players).

Does that mean that you automatically get that player? No, unfortunately, it doesn't. NFL.com (and most sites) keep a list during the season. That list shows the order in which teams get free agents. The list changes based on the standings. The lowest-ranked teams usually get the first picks. That's fair, right? Teams that are struggling should get the chance to get better. It's also, for instance, how the NFL creates the order of the NFL draft.

The bad news is that if someone is ahead of you on the list and wants the same player, then that player goes to your opponent. The good news is that if no one on the list ahead of you wants him, then he's yours. Most sites work their free agent claims the same way.

That means one important thing: **KNOW YOUR DEADLINE!**

The deadline to make free-agent claims is usually Tuesday evening. However, some leagues use different days, so make sure you know. Don't miss a chance at a player because you forgot to put in a claim. (However, after that first deadline, most leagues also allow you to pick up free agents later in the week.)

WHOM TO CUT?

The other part of the free-agent deal is the tougher part. When you want to add a player, you almost always have to cut a player. That can be a tough decision. There's nothing worse than cutting a guy in Week 3 only to watch him blossom into a star in Week 9 . . . for one of your opponents! But that's the chance you have to take.

How do you decide whom to cut? Sometimes, it can be an easy choice. If a player has suffered a season-ending injury or has been demoted, you can cut him with little fear. If a player's team is struggling to score and it is facing a couple of tough defenses, you can let that guy go. Do you have an extra K or TE?

But if you have three running backs and you love all of them and you're trying to add a WR . . . which RB do you cut? This is a tough decision . . . but that's why you're in charge!

REALITY FOOTBALL
FREE AGENTS

In the NFL, free agents are usually signed by teams in the offseason. That is, a player's contract with Team A runs out in January. He can then sign with Team B (though if he's really good, he'll get offers from Teams C, D, E, and F!). In the NFL, teams choose which free agents they WANT to sign, but the players choose which teams they want to join. In fantasy football, it's all up to you!

FREE AGENT TIPS:

Block That Player: Does a fantasy owner in your league have a great running back? Does that RB have a backup on his NFL team? Pick up that backup as free agent. Then if the star RB gets hurt or struggles, your opponent might have to trade with you to get that player's backup. Or not!

Popular Positions: Running back is probably the most important position in fantasy. You can't depend on your two main starters every week. So look for any running backs who are free agents and try to add them. Well . . . good running backs, that is.

Matchup Mania: Some owners switch their defenses and kickers each week based on who those teams are playing in real life. You can try this, but you have to be flexible in case you don't get the player or team that you wanted. The last thing you want is to go into a Sunday without an active player in every spot.

DEALING WITH INJURIES

NFL players train for months and practice all season long between games. They wear tons of protective gear and they take good care of their bodies. However, it's a tough sport and injuries happen. That's bad news for the players and their NFL teams, of course, but it also can affect your fantasy teams. Just like NFL teams have to deal with changes caused by injuries . . . so do you!

One great way to be ready in case of injury is to "handcuff" key players. That means if you draft the Vikings' star running back, you should also draft his backup later. That handcuffs, or links, the two players on your roster. If your star gets injured, you—like his real NFL team—have his backup ready to go.

Another great way to prepare for injuries is to have two solid quarterbacks on your roster. (This is also a good idea because of the bye week; see page 65.) Quarterbacks can miss a game or two with a minor injury, and you don't want to be left without a good point-scoring signal caller.

When you hear that a player has been injured, you should quickly look at the free-agent pool for that position. That will give you a couple of days to research whom you should try to claim to replace him.

REALITY FOOTBALL

THE INJURY REPORT

NFL teams must report all injuries to their players to the league office. This is to be fair to all teams so that everyone knows what players they might be going against when game day rolls around. There are three categories on the injury report. You'll hear and read them during the season, so here is what they generally mean:

Probable: This means that the player's injury is minor and healing and that he is most likely going to play in the upcoming game.

Questionable: The injury is a bit more serious and could very likely prevent the player from playing. If you see this, you should consider if you want to take a chance on whether that player will get a chance to play or not.

Out: This means that a team has said a player will definitely not be playing in the upcoming game. If you see this, you can put that player on your bench and replace him in the active roster.

MAKING TRADES

I'll give you my peanut butter sandwich for that bag of chips.
I'll trade you five green marbles for that one red one.
If you give me three more cookies, I'll give you this juicy apple.

Does this sound like recess or lunchtime at your school? Trading things is nothing new, and trading players in sports is nothing new, either. A team might have too many running backs and need a wide receiver. Another team might have an extra WR and need a RB. Looks like that might be a good trade!

Teams make trades to try to improve their play on the field. That's the most important thing about a trade. They also try not to trade away more than they're getting in return, but that's not as important. In any trade, the main goal is to help your team win.

In fantasy football, you can make trades up until a day or two before the games begin each week. (That's usually a Sunday, but some NFL weeks start on Thursday or Saturday.) NFL.com makes it easy to suggest a trade with a fellow team owner. You can trade players at any position for any other players; you don't have to trade a QB for a QB, for example. However, you must make sure that you have the right players to fill all your positions by the time of the weekend's games. So don't trade away your only tight end without a plan to get one before game time!

Trading is a really fun part of fantasy football. Trades are suggested, rejected, argued over, or just plain booed! Make sure to include trading players on your list of ways to make your fantasy team a winner.

How Trades Happen

Step One: Look over your roster and see what positions need some more strength. Check other teams' rosters for players that would fill that need. Then see who on your team you can part with in exchange.

Step Two: Contact another owner and suggest a trade.

Step Three: This is the fun part. If they say yes, go to Step Four. If they say no, ask them how you can "sweeten" the deal. If they say maybe, then let the trade talkin' begin! Just pretend that you're at lunch trying to get the best sandwich you can.

Step Four: Once you've agreed on a trade, visit your league Web page. From your team's roster page, go to the Trade area. The site will ask you to select the players on each team involved in the trade. Then you send the trade to the Web site.

Step Five: The team you're trading with must go to the Web site and "approve" the trade. Once that's done, the site will place the players on their new teams. It's up to you to make sure they're placed in the right positions before the next game.

TRADE STRATEGIES

Here are some tips to coming up with a good trade . . . as well as how to look at trades that other teams suggest.

- **Remember to focus first on helping your team. Try to make the trade even, but if it's not and it really helps you, don't be afraid to go for it.**

- **Sell it! Don't just say, "I'll give you X for Y." Use facts and stats to show how the trade helps the other guy; it's up to you to know how it will help you!**

- **Look ahead at the NFL schedule. You don't want to make a big trade for a guy only to see that he's on a bye this week!**

- **Got a great player you're trying to trade? Offer him to several teams and see who comes up with the best deal.**

- **Remember what teams your fellow owners love. Many fantasy owners want players from their favorite NFL teams. A Saints' fan, for example, might be more interested in a New Orleans player.**

- **Close but not quite? If someone offers you a trade that you think is pretty close, don't be afraid to send back another idea (called a "counteroffer").**

SAMPLE TRADE OFFERS

Making trades is a combination of art and science. You probably won't be able to complete a trade that isn't fair, but you also don't want to do a trade that helps an opponent too much. Also, remember that some of your fellow owners think differently than you. They might prefer to get a player on the Eagles, for instance, since that's their favorite NFL team. Or they might hate the Rams and never want to get a player from that team. Take advantage of what you know about your fellow owners. Here are some examples of good and bad trade possibilities:

Good:

- The league's No. 5 running back for the No. 3 wide receiver. (RBs are more valuable than WRs in general, but this is pretty even, since the WR is ranked higher than the RB.)
- A very good WR and a decent TE for a very good RB. (This is a good example of how two players can be about equal to one player; this would work especially well if the person trading the RB did not have a good tight end.)

Bad:

- The best QB in the league for two pretty-good wide receivers. (Top QBs are much rarer than mid-level WRs.)
- A top tight end for a very good running back. (RBs will almost always score more than TEs.)

USING WAIVERS

In fantasy football, a free agent is any player who is not drafted. Once the season starts, a player stays a free agent if he is never chosen for a fantasy team. Once he joins a fantasy team, however, he changes a bit.

Here's an example: Say you pick up Joe Fantastic, a wide receiver for the Chiefs. You like Joe and he plays a few games for you, but he's not scoring like you need him to. You decide to cut Joe. Instead of going back into the free-agent pool, for the first week after you cut him he's "on waivers." That means that other fantasy teams can claim him, but that the deadlines are usually longer and the waiver order is different.

Knowing the difference between free agents and waivers is pretty much just watching the deadlines when a player is available. Most sites will have a note right next to the player: "Available Weds after noon EST" or something like that. That means you'll have to wait until Wednesday to put in a claim. After a couple of days, the site will show who got that player.

The main tricky thing about waivers is that they do take longer to be completed. If you really want to add a player from waivers, make sure that there's enough time before the next game to get him put on your roster.

Choosing players on waivers, like free agents, is a combination of great research, careful attention, and a little luck.

Remember, as we said at the beginning of this chapter: Once the draft is over, the real work of putting together a winning team is just beginning!

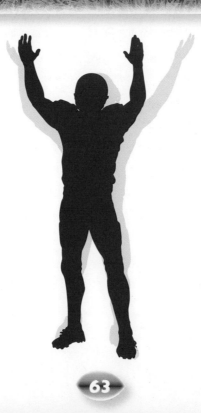

REALITY FOOTBALL
NFL WAIVERS

During an NFL season, if a player with less than four years' experience is cut by a team, he goes on the "waiver wire." That is, he can be signed by another NFL team, but only in a special order. The team that has the poorest record at the time gets first dibs . . . then the order moves up the ranks of teams. If no team claims a player, then he becomes a free agent.

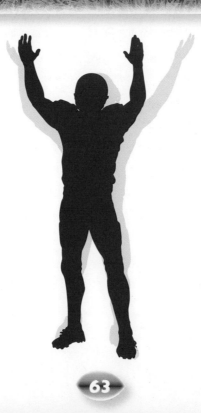

KICKOFF | GETTING | DRAFTING | PLAYING THE GAME | WINNING! | EXTRA

THE SCHEDULE

The fantasy football season mirrors the NFL season, of course. Your players battle new opponents each week. NFL teams face tough games and easier games. They battle division foes and play interconference games. Sometimes they even travel overseas for a game! Your fantasy team always plays online, but you need to be aware of the NFL schedule, too. Make sure you know who is playing on each coming weekend. You'll often have to change around your active roster, depending on what "reality" games are scheduled. (See "Matchups," page 67.)

Another date to remember is Kickoff Weekend. Make sure you know when the NFL is starting its season. Then plan your draft to happen about a week before the first game. That will give your league time to make changes before the first game . . . but also to make sure you know all the key moves that teams are making as they settle on their own rosters.

Don't forget bye weeks, either (see box). They can be a big plus for you or a big minus. Playing them well can make a big difference in your success. It's a good idea to look two or three weeks ahead so that you can make sure to have backups ready for bye weeks, especially for key positions like QB, RB, and WR.

Fantasy football is played with numbers . . . make sure you watch the numbers on the calendar, too.

BYE-WEEK BLUES

NFL teams play 16 games in 17 weeks. Since 1990, the NFL has used "bye weeks" in its schedule. The one week that each team is not scheduled to play is called the "bye." Make sure that you know the bye weeks of all your players. In fact, having too many players on one team can hurt you in this case. If the Colts have a bye in Week 7 and you've got four Colts in your starting lineup, you need to make sure you have four good backups ready! The bye weeks are different for each team each season, so check NFL.com for all the info on each team's bye. If you don't pay attention, you might just be saying "bye-bye" to a chance to win your league! Of course, the flip side of bye weeks is that you might face a fantasy opponent on the week that his star running back's team is back home watching TV instead of playing!

Start or Sit? How to Make Weekly Lineups

You've had a great draft. You've checked out the free agents and added a few key players. You've even watched the waiver wire and found a tight end you really like. Now it's Saturday night and you've got to choose your starting lineup. As fantasy football veterans know, this is the hardest decision of the week. You might have three good running backs on your team and you can only start two of them. How often has this happened? You pick A and B . . . and then C scores 22 points! Aaargh! Most leagues will show you what the players on your bench score each week, too. When that number is a lot, it can be pretty depressing to look at! But that's how it goes in fantasy. You make your picks and then let the games begin.

However, we do have some tips to help you make up those starting lineups.

Deadlines: Make sure you know when your league closes before the games begin. In most leagues, it's just a few minutes before the kickoff in real life. **DON'T FORGET to set your lineup!** You'll kick yourself if you try to switch in a running back at 1:10 and his game has already started. You'll be frozen out!

Bye Weeks: Also, here is yet another reminder to make sure that none of your players is on his team's bye week (see page 65).

Make sure you have an active player in each position. Don't wait until the last minute to find out you have to fill a bye slot.

Matchups: The first thing to look at when setting your lineups is what teams your players' NFL teams are facing. If you have to choose between two running backs, you'll often want to take the one who is playing against the weaker defense. If you're deciding which of your QBs to start, look at how well their opponents defend the pass. NFL teams spend weeks preparing for each opponent; you should learn their lesson and make sure to find out who your fantasy players are facing, too.

FPA: That stands for Fantasy Points Against. For each position, you can find out on NFL.com how many fantasy points a team has allowed. That is, you can see that Team A has let tight ends score 100 points this season, while Team B has allowed only 65 fantasy points to tight ends. That means your tight end will have a tough time against Team B. But can you swap in the tight end who is facing Team A? Knowing how well an NFL team defends each fantasy position can really help you make your lineup decisions.

Previous Games: Another matchup point is how the teams did the first time they played. If you have the Packers' QB, for instance, and he's playing the Bears for the second time in a season, how did he do in their first game? Did Chicago hold him to 6 points? Or did he light up the Bears for 25? It's not an exact science, but looking at a team's previous games will just give you more facts to help your decision.

Injury Issues: Obviously, the first thing is to make sure your players are healthy. Are there any players listed "out" or "questionable"? (See page 57.) They should be put on your bench. But you have to look beyond that. If you have a star wide receiver, is his QB healthy? If a backup or a rookie has to step in, will that WR still be able to score points?

Weather: This is a big factor for kickers and the passing game. In bad weather, such as snow, rain, or wind, kickers will really struggle. If you can change to a kicker playing in good weather (or even better . . . indoors!), you should. Bad weather can also make passing difficult, so maybe you should start your QB playing in the sun over one playing in the snow.

Hunch: Deciding who should start and who should sit is a big part of fantasy football. You take in all the facts you can. You study the matchups and compare stats. You check the injury report and the weather report. You read all the magazines, study the great tips on NFL.com, and watch the reports on TV. After all that, though, sometimes a winning week in fantasy can come down to one thing: You've just got a hunch that a player will bust out with a big week. Got a hunch? Why not give it a try? When it pays off, you'll be psyched that your guy did well . . . and even more excited that you "saw" it coming!

So, that's it. Do all that for 13 or 14 weeks and you'll have a great shot to win your league. And if you do have one of the top records . . . turn the page and find out what's next!

REALITY FOOTBALL

FOOTBALL'S IRON MEN

If you have a few players who are in your starting lineup every week, that's a good sign that your team is doing well. And that those players are doing well and are healthy. In the NFL, it takes a lot of hard work, courage, and luck to play every game, week in and week out. Here are the players who played in the most consecutive games in NFL history, suiting up for their teams no matter what.

352 games
Jeff Feagles, punter

287 games
Brett Favre, quarterback

282 games
Jim Marshall,
defensive tackle

248 games
Morten Andersen,
kicker

69

WINNING!

THE PLAYOFFS!

You did it! You made the playoffs! You assembled a totally awesome team, battled through injuries and tough games, and came out as one of the top four teams.

Now . . . you have more hard work ahead of you.

The fantasy football playoffs are almost a new season themselves. They always happen in the late weeks of the NFL regular season. In most leagues, four teams make the fantasy playoffs. There are two semifinals, then the winners meet in a championship game. Depending on how your league is organized, the championship might be the total of two weeks of games. Why the extra game? That's to make sure that the team that takes home the final trophy is really good enough to dominate over a long time, not just "get lucky" with a great weekend come championship time.

If your league does have the two-week championship, the winner is determined by adding the points for the two weeks. The overall winner has the highest points total. So you might actually lose the first weekend and then come back to win by more points the next week . . . to capture the crown!

Here's a short section on how you can make the most of your playoff opportunity. Just like in the NFL, the intensity is higher, the competition tougher, and the stakes larger. However, just like in the NFL, the playoffs are also more fun!

FANTASY PLAYOFF STRATEGIES

If you think your team has a shot at the playoffs (and you'll probably know by about week 11 or 12), you should start planning ahead. This doesn't mean changing your team's winning formula. You still have to play the rest of the games. In fact, you might need to WIN the rest of the games to make the playoffs. In other words, don't get overconfident. However, that doesn't mean you can't plan for any possibility. There are several important factors to consider as you plan.

GET A GOOD BACKUP QB:

First, this is a good idea in case of injury. If you've depended on your ace QB for a lot of points, and he can't play in the final couple of weekends, you need a good backup. Make a trade, find a free agent, but make sure you're stocked on the bench.

PLAN AHEAD FOR OTHER POSITIONS:

QB is the first to look for since there's usually only one on your starting roster. But the other positions should have backups ready, too, in case of injuries. Keep at least three RBs and WRs on hand.

THE WEEK 16-17 CURSE:

The good part about having star players on NFL-playoff-bound teams is that they score a lot of points for your fantasy team. The bad part is that once those NFL teams earn their own "reality" playoff spots,

NFL coaches sometimes decide to give the stars a rest. We know, they should be thinking of you and your fantasy team, right? Well, not really, but knowing this is key to your playoff survival. If the Colts have clinched a spot, will Peyton Manning play in Week 17? If the Vikings are in, will they rest Adrian Peterson? Every fantasy owner has to deal with this; be sure you're more ready than your opponent!

CHECK THE REAL SCHEDULE:

Knowing who your fantasy players will be playing in real life can be a huge key to the playoffs. This is especially important for the defenses. Make sure that your D is facing an NFL team that is struggling or has been having trouble scoring points. This is an easy way to pile up some playoff points. When choosing your RBs and WRs, see who they're playing, too, and check their FPAs.

WIN GRACEFULLY, LOSE WITH CLASS

Making the playoffs is a great honor for any fantasy team. There were hundreds of choices to make all season long, and you made enough right ones to earn one of the coveted spots. And you'll use the tips we gave you to put together a terrific playoff run.

However, no matter how your playoffs come out, make sure that you're a sportsman. It's frustrating to lose, but you had a good run and earned a playoff spot. You'll be back next year with a fury! And if you're lucky (and good) enough to win, then make sure and not gloat too much (at least not when your fellow owners can hear!). No one likes a rude winner . . . and remember, you want to get these guys in the league again next season, right?

REALITY FOOTBALL

THE "REAL" NFL PLAYOFFS

After the fantasy season is over (that is, after the regular NFL season is over), the NFL playoffs begin (and you can enjoy them without worrying about your fantasy team!). Twelve NFL teams earn spots in the playoffs: the four division winners (North, South, East, and West) in each conference (AFC and NFC), plus two wild-card teams in each conference. The wild-card teams are the non-division-winners with the best overall records. Various tiebreakers are used if teams have the same record.

In each conference, the two division winners with the best overall records get the first playoff weekend off. The other eight teams face off on Wild-Card Weekend. Four winners emerge (two in each conference) to face the top two seeds on Divisional Playoff Weekend. The winners there advance to the Conference Championships. The two conference champs meet, of course, in the Super Bowl.

CELEBRATE!

You won! You won! Dance around with joy, high-five your dog, surprise your mother with a hug, eat ice cream for dinner! (Good luck with that last one!) Wow! After a long season and a tough round of playoffs, you came out on top. You assembled a team of solid starters, mixed and matched your lineup through injuries and trades, and, yes, got a little lucky.

You're a fantasy football champion. Now you have a tiny understanding of what it feels like to win the Super Bowl. And you didn't have to get tackled once!

Even if you didn't win your league, we hope you've enjoyed playing the game. We also hope that this guide has gotten you started in a good way. The rankings section that starts on page 81 is a special guide to the upcoming NFL season. It's packed with rankings and insider info. You'll want to keep it handy all season long. And keep this book handy, too. There are tips you'll need from Draft Day to the championship game.

Now, get out there and "play"!

EXTRA POINTS

FANTASY GLOSSARY

Don't forget to check out the Draft Day glossary on page 41.

Active: describes the players who start for you for each fantasy weekend.

Bench: the players who are in reserve on your fantasy team.

Counteroffer: a suggestion of a change to a trade offer from the team you want to trade with.

Depth chart: a list made by NFL teams showing who are the starters and reserves at each position.

FPA: "fantasy points against"; a measure of how many points an NFL team gives up to one of fantasy football's key positions.

Flex: some leagues offer a roster spot that can be used by an RB or WR or TE, depending on what the owner wants.

Free agent: a player not on the roster of a fantasy (or reality) team.

IR: "injured reserve"; used by NFL teams to indicate that a player is out for the season. If you see a player listed that way, he can't play for that season.

Keeper league: some fantasy leagues let you keep some players from year to year, adding only enough players at the draft to fill your roster.

RBBC: "running back by committee"; when an NFL team uses several running backs, depending on the situation. This makes it tricky for fantasy owners to choose which of those backs to play each week.

Waivers: when a player is cut by a fantasy (or reality) team, he is "waived," and has to be offered to the whole league in order of standings before he can become a free agent.

STAT STOPS
WHERE TO FIND OUT MORE INFORMATION

The Web is the best and fastest place to find fantasy football information. (Make sure to check with your parents whenever you go online.*) You can also read newspapers and magazines, which often have fantasy notes columns. And if you can go to a game in person, that's a terrific way to cheer for your favorite players!

NFL.com: Well, of course, we expect that you'll spend most of your time here. You can go right to the best part (in our humble opinion) by going to www.NFL.com/fantasy. These are the key parts of the NFL.com/Fantasy site that you can use to research your fantasy team and players:

Expert Advice: Michael Fabiano and a host of NFL experts, including some Hall of Fame players, offer daily updates on players to help your team win.

Player Rankings: NFL.com updates the rankings all season long. The site always has the latest updates so your team is always the first to know.

Video: ONLY NFL.com has videos of every player and every key play. Did your top running back score a touchdown? Click here to watch it over and over!

Fantasy 101: If you're just getting started, this is a great way to check up on even more ideas about how to play fantasy.

Plus, check out these other places online for fantasy information:

NFLRush.com

This special site "for kids only" is packed with stuff for young fans. Meet players, see exclusive videos, and check up on fantasy teams and players. There are also online games to play and ideas about staying active and healthy. And speaking of "Reality Football," this site has a ton of videos and articles on how you can play football. You know . . . outdoors? With your friends? You remember.

In addition to all the great information you can find on NFLRush.com, there's also a special fantasy game just for kids. The NFL-Rush game is a great way to play fantasy. You don't even have to worry about a draft! You choose a lineup of players every week during the season, watch them play and score . . . and have a chance to win really cool prizes!

Team Sites

Each NFL team also runs its own Web site. These can be a great place to learn even more about players. Check the "News" tabs or "Press" tabs for articles and blogs about the season and about player moves.

sikids.com

Sports Illustrated Kids magazine has lots of great information on the NFL, fantasy football, and NFL players, all written for kids to enjoy.

Parents: We checked these sites to make sure they're okay for kids. However, always monitor the sites your kids visit to make sure they surf safely.

HOW TO READ
THE RANKINGS

On the opposite page, we begin our special section for this upcoming NFL season. It includes rankings of the top players at the key fantasy positions. We start off with a list from NFL.com of the top 100 players (at any position). Sometimes it's best just to pick the best available player regardless of position.

Then we move on to position-by-position lists, including quick capsules of top players at each position. Remember that these are not absolutely complete. Players change teams, teams change strategies, and the season's results change everything! But this is a great start, and a terrific way to help plan your draft strategy. Check out the special "Sleepers" section for most positions (but don't tell your friends…ssshhh!), and there's even a quick look at how some famous rookies fit into the fantasy football plan for this season.

Like a football Santa, you have to make your lists (you can start with ours) and check them twice . . . and pick the players you think will be nice.

Good luck!

2010 NFL.COM FANTASY FOOTBALL GUIDE

Note: All information up to date as of press date; please check NFL.com for updates and the latest news.

THE TOP 100

1. Chris Johnson, Titans, **RB**
2. Adrian Peterson, Vikings **RB**
3. Aaron Rodgers, Packers **QB**
4. Drew Brees, Saints **QB**
5. Maurice Jones-Drew, Jaguars **RB**
6. Peyton Manning, Colts **QB**
7. Ray Rice, Ravens **RB**
8. Michael Turner, Falcons **RB**
9. Andre Johnson, Texans **WR**
10. Frank Gore, 49ers **RB**
11. Rashard Mendenhall, Steelers **RB**
12. Steven Jackson, Rams **RB**
13. Tom Brady, Patriots **QB**
14. Larry Fitzgerald, Cardinals **WR**
15. Cedric Benson, Bengals **RB**
16. Philip Rivers, Chargers **QB**
17. Jamaal Charles, Chiefs **RB**
18. Randy Moss, Patriots **WR**
19. DeAngelo Williams, Panthers **RB**
20. Ryan Grant, Packers **RB**
21. Reggie Wayne, Colts **WR**
22. DeSean Jackson, Eagles **WR**
23. Miles Austin, Cowboys **WR**
24. Matt Schaub, Texans **QB**
25. Calvin Johnson, Lions **WR**
26. Tony Romo, Cowboys **QB**
27. Knowshon Moreno, Broncos **RB**
28. Roddy White, Falcons **WR**
29. Vincent Jackson, Chargers **WR**
30. Brandon Marshall, Dolphins **WR**
31. Marques Colston, Saints **WR**
32. LeSean McCoy, Eagles **RB**
33. Felix Jones, Cowboys **RB**
34. Shonn Greene, Jets **RB**
35. Sidney Rice, Vikings **WR**
36. Brett Favre, Vikings **QB**
37. Steve Smith, Giants **WR**
38. Greg Jennings, Packers **WR**
39. Anquan Boldin, Ravens **WR**
40. Dallas Clark, Colts **TE**
41. Joseph Addai, Colts **RB**
42. Beanie Wells, Cardinals **RB**
43. Antonio Gates, Chargers **TE**
44. Ronnie Brown, Dolphins **RB**
45. Steve Smith, Panthers **WR**
46. Vernon Davis, 49ers **TE**
47. Jonathan Stewart, Panthers **RB**
48. Pierre Thomas, Saints **RB**
49. Ryan Mathews, Chargers **RB**
50. Chad Ochocinco, Bengals **WR**

Some fantasy owners like to just pick the best player available, no matter what position. Here's a list of the top 100 fantasy players for 2010. You can use it as a checklist to make sure you've researched all the best players.

51. Jay Cutler, Bears QB

52. Matt Forté, Bears RB

53. Eli Manning, Giants QB

54. Brandon Jacobs, Giants RB

55. Brent Celek, Eagles TE

56. Clinton Portis, Redskins RB

57. Ben Tate, Texans RB

58. Leon Washington, Seahawks RB

59. Jason Witten, Cowboys TE

60. Marion Barber, Cowboys RB

61. Dwayne Bowe, Chiefs WR

62. Donovan McNabb, Redskins QB

63. Tony Gonzalez, Falcons TE

64. Kevin Kolb, Eagles QB

65. Hines Ward, Steelers WR

66. Joe Flacco, Ravens QB

67. Matt Ryan, Falcons QB

68. Percy Harvin, Vikings WR

69. Jerome Harrison, Browns RB

70. Fred Jackson, Bills RB

71. Wes Welker, Patriots WR

72. Mike Sims-Walker, Jaguars WR

73. Robert Meachem, Saints WR

74. Michael Crabtree, 49ers WR

75. Jermichael Finley, Packers TE

76. Mike Wallace, Steelers WR

77. Jahvid Best, Lions RB

78. Hakeem Nicks, Giants WR

79. Santana Moss, Redskins WR

80. Vince Young, Titans QB

81. C.J. Spiller, Bills RB

82. Pierre Garcon, Colts WR

83. Owen Daniels, Texans TE

84. Ben Roethlisberger, Steelers QB

85. Chris Cooley, Redskins TE

86. Jeremy Maclin, Eagles WR

87. Carnell Williams, Buccaneers RB

88. Derrick Mason, Ravens WR

89. Steve Breaston, Cardinals WR

90. Darren McFadden, Raiders RB

91. Ahmad Bradshaw, Giants RB

92. Carson Palmer, Bengals QB

93. LaDainian Tomlinson, Jets RB

94. Thomas Jones, Chiefs RB

95. Chester Taylor, Bears RB

96. Ricky Williams, Dolphins RB

97. Donald Driver, Packers WR

98. Reggie Bush, Saints RB

99. Kellen Winslow, Browns TE

100. Visanthe Shiancoe, Vikings TE

QUARTERBACKS

TOP 30

1. Aaron Rodgers, Green Bay
2. Drew Brees, New Orleans
3. Peyton Manning, Indianapolis
4. Tom Brady, New England
5. Philip Rivers, San Diego
6. Matt Schaub, Houston
7. Tony Romo, Dallas
8. Brett Favre, Minnesota
9. Jay Cutler, Chicago
10. Eli Manning, N.Y. Giants
11. Donovan McNabb, Washington
12. Kevin Kolb, Philadelphia
13. Joe Flacco, Baltimore
14. Matt Ryan, Atlanta
15. Vince Young, Tennessee
16. Ben Roethlisberger, Pittsburgh
17. Carson Palmer, Cincinnati
18. Alex Smith, San Francisco
19. Matt Cassel, Kansas City
20. Mark Sanchez, N.Y. Jets
21. Chad Henne, Miami
22. Jason Campbell, Oakland
23. David Garrard, Jacksonville
24. Matthew Stafford, Detroit
25. Matt Leinart, Arizona
26. Kyle Orton, Denver
27. Matt Hasselbeck, Seattle
28. Matt Moore, Carolina
29. Josh Freeman, Tampa Bay
30. Jake Delhomme, Cleveland

DRAFT STRATEGY

You need to leave your draft with a top-notch quarterback. The best ones score a lot of points every week. One of your top two picks should be one of the top passers. The NFL has seen a huge rise in passing in recent years. In 2009, more passers threw for more than 4,000 yards and for 25 or more touchdowns than ever before. That's a lot of fantasy points! Look for a solid backup quarterback after Round 7 or 8 in the draft, too. Also, it's a rare rookie QB who shines in fantasy football.

1 ## Aaron Rodgers, Green Bay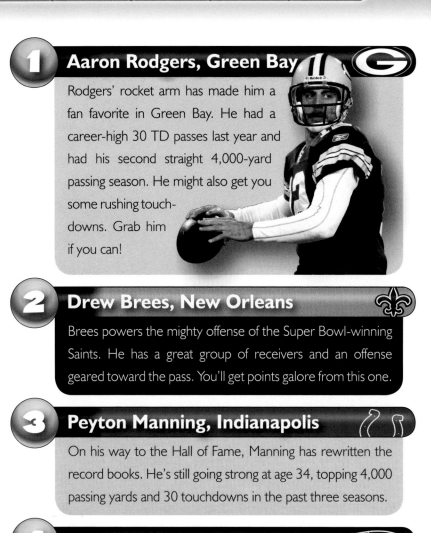

Rodgers' rocket arm has made him a fan favorite in Green Bay. He had a career-high 30 TD passes last year and had his second straight 4,000-yard passing season. He might also get you some rushing touchdowns. Grab him if you can!

2 ## Drew Brees, New Orleans

Brees powers the mighty offense of the Super Bowl-winning Saints. He has a great group of receivers and an offense geared toward the pass. You'll get points galore from this one.

3 ## Peyton Manning, Indianapolis

On his way to the Hall of Fame, Manning has rewritten the record books. He's still going strong at age 34, topping 4,000 passing yards and 30 touchdowns in the past three seasons.

4 ## Tom Brady, New England

The season after his knee injury, Brady wasted no time in reclaiming his spot among the best. He was over 4,000 yards and had 28 TD passes, and figures to do even better in 2010.

5 Philip Rivers, San Diego

Rivers led the Chargers to 13 wins while setting new career bests for passing yards and touchdown passes. He has raised his passing yards totals in each of the past three years. San Diego loves to pass; this strong-armed QB is the reason why.

6 Matt Schaub, Houston

Guess who led the NFL in passing yards in 2009? Not Manning, Brees, or Rodgers. It was this young up-and-coming star. He had nine games with 300 or more passing yards.

7 Tony Romo, Dallas

Romo set two career marks last season that mean good things ahead for his fantasy owners. He threw for more passing yards than ever (4,483) while only throwing 9 picks.

8 Brett Favre, Minnesota

Put a big asterisk next to this one. Make sure to check back on NFL.com/Fantasy to see if this all-time superstar is coming back . . . again. If he does, look for good things in 2010.

9 Jay Cutler, Chicago

The best news for fantasy owners looking to pick Cutler is the Bears' new offensive coach. Mike Martz loves to pass more than a NASCAR driver. His plan for the run-heavy Bears is to open up passing lanes for Cutler to rack up the points!

10 Eli Manning, NY Giants

The "other" Manning posted career highs in passing yards and touchdowns in 2009. He has a great group of young receivers, too.

11 Donovan McNabb, Washington

McNabb finds a new home in D.C. after a great career with the Eagles. He adds running power (and some rushing TDs) to veteran passing skills.

12 Kevin Kolb, Philadelphia

Kolb takes over for McNabb in Philadelphia, and fans there expect a lot. In two starts in 2009, he threw for a total of 718 yards and 4 touchdowns!

13 Joe Flacco, Baltimore

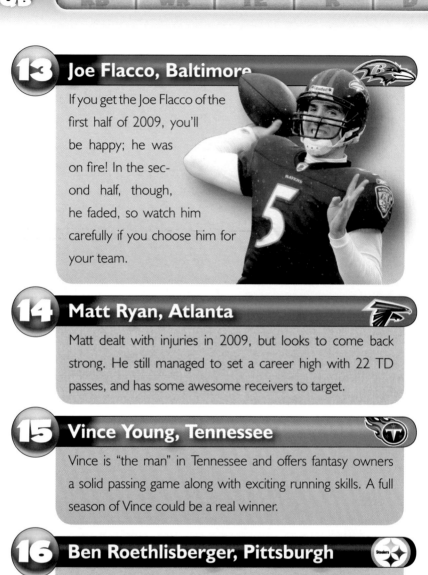

If you get the Joe Flacco of the first half of 2009, you'll be happy; he was on fire! In the second half, though, he faded, so watch him carefully if you choose him for your team.

14 Matt Ryan, Atlanta

Matt dealt with injuries in 2009, but looks to come back strong. He still managed to set a career high with 22 TD passes, and has some awesome receivers to target.

15 Vince Young, Tennessee

Vince is "the man" in Tennessee and offers fantasy owners a solid passing game along with exciting running skills. A full season of Vince could be a real winner.

16 Ben Roethlisberger, Pittsburgh

Big Ben will miss some games at the start of the 2010 season because of a league suspension. If you pick him, pick someone else to start the season for you.

17 Carson Palmer, Cincinnati

The Bengals switched to a run-heavy offense in 2009, and that hurt Carson's value as a fantasy player. He still has great talent, though, and would be a good backup for you.

18 Alex Smith, San Francisco

You might not want to depend on Alex for fantasy points every week, but against some teams, he could be a solid points-scorer.

19 Matt Cassel, Kansas City

With a full year as the Chiefs' starter, Matt has the talent and teammates to really shine in 2010. Watch him in the early going and snap him up as a free agent.

20 Mark Sanchez, NY Jets

Yes, Mark led the Jets to the AFC Championship Game as a rookie, but he only threw 12 TDs in the regular season. New receivers might help him take another step forward.

SLEEPERS

Here are some young passers who might be on the rise in 2010. No, they're not ALL named "Matt."

- **Matt Leinart, Arizona** • **Matthew Stafford, Detroit**
- **Matt Moore, Carolina** • **Sam Bradford, St. Louis**

RUNNING BACKS

TOP 30

1. **Chris Johnson, Tennessee**
2. **Adrian Peterson, Minnesota**
3. **Maurice Jones-Drew, Jacksonville**
4. **Ray Rice, Baltimore**
5. **Michael Turner, Atlanta**
6. **Frank Gore, San Francisco**
7. **Rashard Mendenhall, Pittsburgh**
8. **Steven Jackson, St. Louis**
9. **Cedric Benson, Cincinnati**
10. **Jamaal Charles, Kansas City**
11. **DeAngelo Williams, Carolina**
12. **Ryan Grant, Green Bay**
13. **Knowshon Moreno, Denver**
14. **LeSean McCoy, Philadelphia**
15. **Felix Jones, Dallas**
16. **Shonn Greene, N.Y. Jets**
17. **Joseph Addai, Indianapolis**
18. **Beanie Wells, Arizona**
19. **Ronnie Brown, Miami**
20. **Jonathan Stewart, Carolina**
21. **Pierre Thomas, New Orleans**
22. **Ryan Mathews, San Diego**
23. **Matt Forté, Chicago**
24. **Brandon Jacobs, N.Y. Giants**
25. **Clinton Portis, Washington**
26. **Ben Tate, Houston**
27. **Leon Washington, Seattle**
28. **Marion Barber, Dallas**
29. **Jerome Harrison, Cleveland**
30. **Fred Jackson, Buffalo**

DRAFT STRATEGY

You need two good running backs to succeed in fantasy football. Chances are you'll get a shot at one of the top six or eight backs; the key is to find that really solid second running back. Look for players who score on runs and passes and who are a big part of their teams' offense. Some stars on new teams might have found a new place to shine. And several players are set to be the short-yardage backs; those guys won't get yardage, but they will get TDs. Several rookie runners might emerge this year, too.

1 Chris Johnson, Tennessee

Chris was the leading scorer in fantasy football last year and shows no signs of slowing down. The Titans give him all the work he can handle, and he will often be the player chosen first in fantasy drafts this year. Good luck getting him!

2 Adrian Peterson, Minnesota

If you thought A.P. was good before, he got even better in 2009. Be sure to grab this star if you can to watch him continue to add to his legend.

3 Maurice Jones-Drew, Jacksonville

The man they call "Mo-Jo" came through in a big way in his first full season as the starter for the Jags. He set career highs in rushing yards and touchdowns in 2009.

4 Ray Rice, Baltimore

Rice's all-around skills (he caught 78 passes in 2009) make him very valuable, while his breakaway speed means any carry could turn into a long gain.

5 Michael Turner, Atlanta

Turner had a huge year in 2008, but slowed down in 2009. Having less work will make him fresher heading into 2010, so grab this all-around runner if you can.

6 Frank Gore, San Francisco

With a solid passing game growing in S.F., the power running of Frank Gore will have more room to shine. He's coming off his best season since 2006, too.

7 Rashard Mendenhall, Pittsburgh

With a full season as the Steelers' starter, Rashard could emerge as a big star in 2010. His early weeks will be helped by the suspension of Ben Roethlisberger, too.

8 Steven Jackson, St. Louis

Jackson benefits from being the main runner in almost all of the Rams' formations. He racked up more than 1,400 yards last year on a team that will have to run a lot.

9 Cedric Benson, Cincinnati

On a Bengals team that focuses on running the ball, Cedric took full advantage. He set a career high with 1,251 yards in 2009, and figures to do even better in 2010.

10 Jamaal Charles, Kansas City

Fantasy fans took notice of Jamaal's great final few weeks of 2009, in which he was one of fantasy's top scorers. Quick, young, and talented, Jamaal could turn into one of the NFL's most high-scoring RBs.

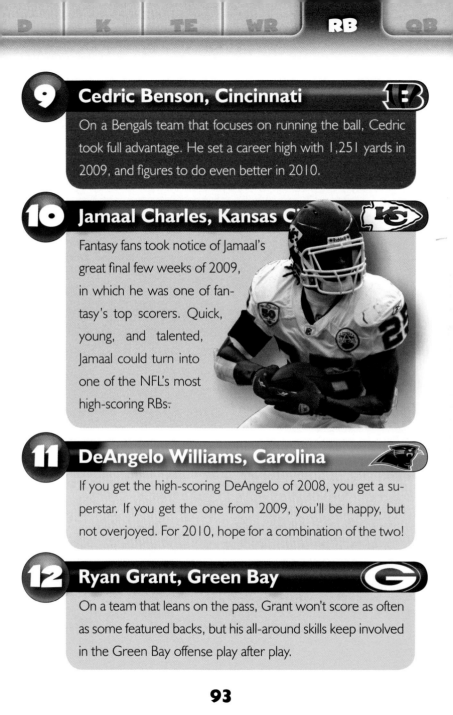

11 DeAngelo Williams, Carolina

If you get the high-scoring DeAngelo of 2008, you get a superstar. If you get the one from 2009, you'll be happy, but not overjoyed. For 2010, hope for a combination of the two!

12 Ryan Grant, Green Bay

On a team that leans on the pass, Grant won't score as often as some featured backs, but his all-around skills keep involved in the Green Bay offense play after play.

13 Knowshon Moreno, Denver

In 2009, Knowshon gained 1,160 yards and ran for 9 TDs as a rookie. He figures to continue that success in 2010. He'll split time with other runners, but his youth and speed will give him the edge. He'd be a solid No. 2 runner.

14 LeSean McCoy, Philadelphia

With the departure of veteran Brian Westbrook from the Eagles, LeSean moves into the full-time starting role. A solid 2009 season signals good times ahead in Philly.

15 Felix Jones, Dallas

If you got fantasy points for excitement, Felix would be No. 1. His speed and outside moves helped him earn the starting spot in Big D for 2010.

16 Shonn Greene, N.Y. Jets

A fantastic playoff run put Greene in the spotlight for 2010, especially with the departure of 2009 starter Thomas Jones to Kansas City. Will Shonn fly on the Jets?

17 Joseph Addai, Indianapolis

Peyton Manning does the heavy lifting, but there's lots left for Joseph to do. He scored 13 touchdowns in 2009, and he also has great pass-catching skills.

18 Beanie Wells, Arizona

As a rookie, Beanie showed what he could do in the second half of the year. If he emerges as a starter in Arizona, snap him up—he could be a really good one.

18 Ronnie Brown, Miami

If not for an injured foot in 2009, this veteran runner would have ranked higher than here. His versatility, especially in the "Wildcat" formation, make him worth a look.

20 Jonathan Stewart, Carolina

Big, fast, strong: Jonathan is all those things. He scored 10 TDs in 2009 and will make the choice between him and DeAngelo Williams hard for Panthers' coaches.

21 Pierre Thomas, New Orleans

Pierre has a lot of talent, but he also has a lot of competition for the football on the Saints. If he gets his chances, though, he can score points both running and catching passes.

22 Ryan Mathews, San Diego

This rookie has big shoes to fill in San Diego, but it looks like he has the all-around talent (speed, great moves, power) to take over for the Hall-of-Famer "L.T."

23 Matt Forté, Chicago

Matt had a bit of a "sophomore slump" (that is, a second season not as good as his first). Competition from Chester Taylor might inspire Matt to put up good numbers again, though.

24 Brandon Jacobs, N.Y. Giants

Like many backs, Brandon will compete for carries, in his case from speedy Ahmad Bradshaw. But he has the skills to find the end zone, which he did 15 times in 2008.

25 Clinton Portis, Washington

Will the arrival of Donovan McNabb inspire this veteran to bounce back? Injuries and age have slowed him, but a new energy in D.C. might just rub off on him in 2010.

26 Ben Tate, Houston

The Texans have a great passing attack, thanks to Matt Schaub. They hope this powerful rookie is the answer to their ground game, though Ben will fight for carries with Steve Slaton.

27 Leon Washington, Seattle

Leon comes over from the Jets, where he showed speed and an ability to make tacklers miss. He'll be one of several players new coach Pete Carroll will look to for rushing yards.

28 Marion Barber, Dallas

While defenses flock to try to catch Felix Jones, Marion might just slip in there to snag a handful of touchdowns near the goal line. A veteran, he'll be a good balance for Jones' speed.

SLEEPERS

Here are some runners who might get overlooked on Draft Day. They might be a good late-round pick for you.

- **C.J. Spiller, Buffalo** • **Chester Taylor, Chicago**
- **Thomas Jones, Kansas City** • **Carnell Williams, Tampa Bay**

WIDE RECEIVERS

TOP 30

1. **Andre Johnson, Houston**
2. **Larry Fitzgerald, Arizona**
3. **Randy Moss, New England**
4. **Reggie Wayne, Indianapolis**
5. **DeSean Jackson, Philadelphia**
6. **Miles Austin, Dallas**
7. **Calvin Johnson, Detroit**
8. **Roddy White, Atlanta**
9. **Vincent Jackson, San Diego**
10. **Brandon Marshall, Miami**
11. **Marques Colston, New Orleans**
12. **Sidney Rice, Minnesota**
13. **Steve Smith, N.Y. Giants**
14. **Greg Jennings, Green Bay**
15. **Anquan Boldin, Baltimore**
16. **Steve Smith, Carolina**
17. **Chad Ochocinco, Cincinnati**
18. **Dwayne Bowe, Kansas City**
19. **Hines Ward, Pittsburgh**
20. **Percy Harvin, Minnesota**
21. **Wes Welker, New England**
22. **Mike Sims-Walker, Jacksonville**
23. **Robert Meacham, New Orleans**
24. **Michael Crabtree, San Francisco**
25. **Mike Wallace, Pittsburgh**
26. **Hakeem Nicks, N.Y. Giants**
27. **Santana Moss, Washington**
28. **Pierre Garcon, Indianapolis**
29. **Jeremy Maclin, Philadelphia**
30. **Derrick Mason, Baltimore**

DRAFT STRATEGY

This is one position where patience pays off. If you don't get one of the three or four superstar wide receivers, you'll still have plenty of very good players from which to choose. Chances are good that if you can wait, you'll fill your other positions with stars and then find two solid WRs for your lineup. However, there's also nothing wrong with trying to snag one of those big three or four, players who will almost surely rack up points every week. It's a passing league now, and WRs really benefit.

1 · Andre Johnson, Houston

With seven games of 20 or more fantasy points in 2009, Andre is the only wide receiver who is worth a first-round pick. His size, speed, and pass-catching ability, along with his hot young QB Matt Schaub, have made him a star.

2 · Larry Fitzgerald, Arizona

The only question about Larry, who is blessed with size and great leaping ability, is whether the loss of fellow WR Anquan Boldin will mean defenses can focus on him more often.

3 · Randy Moss, New England

One of the most gifted receivers of all time, Randy is showing that some things get better with age. He topped 10 TDs for the third straight season and should shine again in 2010.

4 · Reggie Wayne, Indianapolis

With 35 TD catches in the past four seasons, Reggie has become a solid scorer. He figures to be your number-one wide receiver if he's available.

5 DeSean Jackson, Philadelphia

DeSean burst onto the NFL scene in 2009 with several super-long scoring plays that excited fans and fantasy owners. He'll be the key target of the Eagles' new starting QB, Kevin Kolb, and will see a lot of attention on Draft Day.

6 Miles Austin, Dallas

Miles was a big surprise last year, scoring 11 TDs after starting the year on the bench. He'll be no surprise in 2010; expect him to be gone early in your draft.

7 Calvin Johnson, Detroit

Calvin had a down year for him, but with his talent, he won't stay down long. And with QB Matthew Stafford another year older and wiser, Calvin's numbers should go back up.

8 Roddy White, Atlanta

Roddy has improved his numbers in each of the past three seasons, and with QB Matt Ryan settling into his star role, Roddy will probably keep that streak alive.

9 | Vincent Jackson, San Diego

The one thing that a strong-armed passer like San Diego's Philip Rivers needs is a go-to guy. That's Vincent, one of the largest regular WRs in the league. He set career highs in catches and TDs in 2009.

10 | Brandon Marshall, Miami

Despite missing four games, Brandon still topped 1,000 receiving yards in 2009. In Miami, he'll be the No. 1 receiver in a creative and possibly high-scoring offense.

11 | Marques Colston, New Orleans

The Saints' Drew Brees has a lot of great options to throw to, but Marques is one of his favorites. He has had at least 70 catches for 1,000 yards in each of the last three seasons.

12 | Sidney Rice, Minnesota

This is tricky: If Brett Favre comes back to the Vikings, Sidney will surely have another monster season. If Favre retires (again!), Sidney might struggle to post good numbers.

13 | **Steve Smith, N.Y. Gian** | ny

The Giants have been playing since 1925 but no Giants receiver ever had more catches than Steve's 107 last year. In an offense that's starting to pass more, he has become the favorite target for QB Eli Manning.

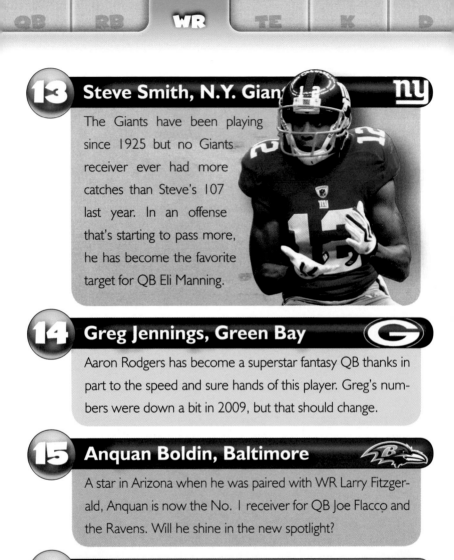

14 | **Greg Jennings, Green Bay** | G

Aaron Rodgers has become a superstar fantasy QB thanks in part to the speed and sure hands of this player. Greg's numbers were down a bit in 2009, but that should change.

15 | **Anquan Boldin, Baltimore**

A star in Arizona when he was paired with WR Larry Fitzgerald, Anquan is now the No. 1 receiver for QB Joe Flacco and the Ravens. Will he shine in the new spotlight?

16 | **Steve Smith, Carolina**

This Steve Smith has a long and successful career behind him. Whether he has a good year ahead will depend on how well new starting QB Matt Moore and he click.

17 Chad Ochocinco, Cincinnati

You might hear his name more on Twitter or on a reality show, but fantasy owners know he's the real deal on the field. He has seven 1,000-yard seasons and has scored 8 or more TDs in five seasons. His only issue will be Cincy's focus on running.

18 Dwayne Bowe, Kansas City

With his skills and speed, more is expected of this young pass catcher. With another season of connecting with Matt Cassel, maybe this is the year Bowe breaks out.

19 Hines Ward, Pittsburgh

Hines is the battery bunny of the NFL: He just keeps going and going. Entering his 13th season, he has caught at least 70 passes and 6 touchdowns each of the past four years.

20 Percy Harvin, Minnesota

Percy connected early and often with Brett Favre in 2009. If Favre comes back, Percy's rise will continue. If Favre "retires," Harvin will struggle to take catches from Sidney Rice.

21 Wes Welker, New England

Watch Wes carefully in training camp. He suffered a knee injury in the final game of 2009. If he's recovered, he's a very valuable target for Tom Brady and will catch a ton of passes.

22 Mike Sims-Walker, Jacksonville

Mike is the No. 1 receiver on the Jaguars and set career highs in receptions, receiving yards, and touchdowns in 2009. He has the talent and size to become a big-time receiver in the NFL. The question is: Can QB David Garrard get him the ball enough?

23 Robert Meacham, New Orleans

Robert is a good No. 2 or No. 3 option for QB Drew Brees, and he could do the same for your team. He had only 45 catches, but 9 went for TDs.

24 Michael Crabtree, San Francisco

This could be a real breakout year for this young player. His speed makes him tough to cover. If he and QB Alex Smith can start clicking, he could become a big star.

25 Mike Wallace, Pittsburgh

The move of Santonio Holmes to the Jets makes Mike the No. 2 receiver on a Steelers' team that *looooves* to pass. His size makes him a great target for Pittsburgh QBs.

26 Hakeem Nicks, N.Y. Giants

In only his first year, Hakeem improved game after game and was putting up big numbers at the end of the year. If that trend continues, he could be a high-scoring part of your team.

27 Santana Moss, Washington

Santana's numbers have been falling, but the addition of strong-armed QB Donovan McNabb could put this veteran back among the elite in the NFL.

28 Pierre Garcon, Indianapolis

Injuries to other receivers gave Pierre a chance to shine, especially in the playoffs. That could be the boost he needs to play a big part in the Colts' active passing offense.

SLEEPERS

There is always a big group of wide receivers who seem ready to emerge into starting spots. Keep an eye on these players.

- **Devin Thomas, Washington** • **Johnny Knox, Chicago**
- **Julian Edelman, New England** • **Joshua Cribbs, Cleveland**

TIGHT ENDS

TOP 10

DRAFT STRATEGY

You need to pick one, but you don't need to spend a high draft pick on a TE. If you don't get solid receivers, draft your TE earlier.

1 Dallas Clark, Indianapolis

He just keeps getting better! Dallas' reception and yardage totals have gone up every year since 2006. He and QB Peyton Manning see eye to eye.

2 Antonio Gates, San Diego

His size makes him hard to cover; his soft hands make him a QB's dream. His fantasy points make him a TE to target!

3 Vernon Davis, San Francisco

Don't expect Vernon to match his NFL-record 13 TDs, but do expect him to put up big numbers for you.

4 Brent Celek, Philadelphia

With career bests in all categories in 2009, Brent looks like a real rising star at this position.

5 Jason Witten, Dallas

He makes a lot of catches, but hasn't scored as much as Dallas fans had hoped; maybe this will be his year for TDs.

6 Tony Gonzalez, Atlanta

One of the best TEs ever, Tony gives young QB Matt Ryan a reliable target and gives fantasy owners a ton of points.

7 Jermichael Finley, Green Bay

Jermichael came on strong at the end of the season, giving him a rocket boost into fantasy stardom in 2010.

8 Owen Daniels, Houston

If he can come back from a knee injury, Owen has the talent to become one of the top players at this position.

9 Chris Cooley, Washington

Chris hopes to come back from an ankle injury to take advantage of new QB Donovan McNabb, who loves TEs.

KICKERS

TOP 10

1. **Stephen Gostkowski, New England**
2. **Garrett Hartley, New Orleans**
3. **Nate Kaeding, San Diego**
4. **David Akers, Philadelphia**
5. **Mason Crosby, Green Bay**
6. **Ryan Longwell, Minnesota**
7. **Rob Bironas, Tennessee**
8. **Matt Prater, Denver**
9. **Lawrence Tynes, N.Y. Giants**
10. **Kris Brown, Houston**

DRAFT STRATEGY

Aiming for a kicker from a high-scoring team (or who plays indoors) is a good start. Avoid kickers from bad-weather teams.

1 Stephen Gostkowski, New England

Stephen has been in the top three among kickers each of the past three seasons. With New England's powerful offense, that doesn't figure to change.

2 Garrett Hartley, New Orleans

A Super Bowl hero for the Saints, he's ready to pick up where he left off in the playoffs and have a big year.

3 Nate Kaeding, San Diego

On the other hand, Kaeding is hoping to put his playoff misses behind him and get back to being a steady performer.

4 David Akers, Philadelphia

Two straight seasons with 140 points, a powerful leg for long FGs, and a great offense: He's in good shape to score big.

5 Mason Crosby, Green Bay

Mason's success argues against avoiding bad-weather kickers. He's been in the top five among kickers three times.

6 Ryan Longwell, Minnesota

He had a great season with Brett Favre at QB; if Favre doesn't come back, Longwell might score even more points.

7 Rob Bironas, Tennessee

Strong and accurate, he once kicked eight FGs in one game! He won't do that every week, but look for him to score a lot.

8 Matt Prater, Denver

Denver will score a lot of points this year, and Matt will get more than his share.

9 Lawrence Tynes, N.Y. Giants

With Eli Manning leading a great "Jints" offense, Lawrence has become one of fantasy's best-scoring kickers.

DEFENSES

TOP 15

DRAFT STRATEGY

Some teams, like Minnesota and Baltimore, have been steady point-scorers on defense. New Orleans and the Jets are on the rise, though. Draft a defense you can play the first few weeks with, then figure you'll change based on matchups.

1 New York Jets

The Jets allowed the fewest points in the NFL last year, thanks in part to great CBs.

2 Minnesota Vikings

For some reason, the Vikings always seem to score a lot of interception and fumble return TDs—it'll be true again in '10.

3 Philadelphia Eagles

The Eagles score well in sacks, but also, thanks to DeSean Jackson, are huge in the return game.

4 Green Bay Packers

Cornerback Charles Woodson was the Defensive Player of the Year, but he's not the only star on this very tough D.

5 Baltimore Ravens

The Ravens are always among the top Ds. Star LB Ray Lewis is a big reason, but a stingy secondary plays a key part.

6 Pittsburgh Steelers

Welcome back, Troy Polamalu! The All-Pro safety missed most of 2009; with him back, the Steel Curtain is back, too!

7 New Orleans Saints

A big reason for the Saints' run to the Super Bowl title was a ball-hawking defense that scored 9 TDs.

8 San Francisco 49ers

With a Hall of Fame LB (Mike Singletary) as the head coach and led by an All-Pro LB (Patrick Willis), the 49ers are A-OK.

GENERATION NEXT!

Here's a look at some of the NFL rookies who might play a big part in fantasy football this year.

Ryan Mathews, RB, San Diego

Ryan takes over from the great LaDainian Tomlinson. Ryan had a star career at Fresno State and has speed and great cutback ability. He's sure to get a lot of touches.

Jahvid Best, RB, Detroit

On a team that really strugged on offense, Jahvid might be the answer at running back. He has breakaway speed and great moves.

Dez Bryant, WR, Dallas

A great minicamp just proved what many were saying—that Bryant was one of the most exciting players in the 2010 draft.

Ben Tate, RB, Houston

Boom, boom, boom. That's the sound you'll hear when Big Ben carries the ball. He'll be a big, powerful runner in Texas.

Sam Bradford, QB, St. Louis

The Rams have handed the reins to Sam, so it's up to him to perform. Rookie QBs rarely make a big fantasy impact, though.